The Educated English

In the Brave Days of Old

Macaulay's
The Lays of Ancient Rome

read, and with introductions and epilogue, by

Peter Greenhalgh

First published 2012
English Speech and Pronunciation Limited
Westwood House, Highcross Road,
Southfleet, Kent, DA13 9PH, England.
www.speechandpronunciation.com

Typeset by Patrick Armstrong, Book Production Services
www.pabs.co.uk

Printed and bound in Great Britain by Direct POD
www.direct-pod.com

ISBN 978–1–908001–07–8

Contents

The Illustrations

The illustrations are the work of **John Reinhard Weguelin** (1849–1927), an English artist who specialised in classical and romantic themes and is well known both as an illustrator and as the painter of such fine works as *Lesbia*, *The Bath*, and *The Mermaid of Zennor*.

The Recording

The recording begins with the introduction "Macaulay, *The Lays* and *Horatius*", the text of which begins on page 5.

The *Educated English* series

This delightful new series of audiobooks has been designed to provide, conveniently and inexpensively, the delight of listening to English prose, verse and songs that are all well read or sung with a good English accent. The series will include stories, poems, rhymes and songs on many themes, for all ages and from and about many lands. There will be a variety of old favourites and less known pieces, but all will share the virtue of being recorded by readers or singers with a good Standard English accent.

Every title in the series is presented with both text and audio recording so that you can both read and listen to everything. You can just enjoy the audio while driving the car or luxuriating in a hot bath or lying in bed or on the beach; or you can read the text while listening, which is particularly valuable for those learning or seeking to improve their English either as children or as students whose first language is not English. Besides, so many of the works in the series cry out to be read aloud, so you can not only enjoy hearing them read to you but read them out loud yourself, either to your children or just to yourself for the sheer pleasure of getting your tongue round the luscious language.

It is not only enjoyable but important to be able to listen to these gems of English prose and verse beautifully read by readers with a good pronunciation. We live in a decadent time with seemingly ever-declining standards of education and both written and spoken English. The present generation in England has been called the "innit" generation because that is how so many of our ill-taught "youf" pronounce "isn't it?" English is a language of great power and beauty, one of the richest and most subtle forms of communication the human race has ever devised. It has also become the international language. Like the family silver it needs to be cherished and kept polished, not allowed to get dented and stained and ugly. Yet even the BBC has put away the silver-cloth.

Even its supposedly high-quality channels, and particularly the World Services where clarity of speech and pronunciation are especially important, have been debased to the point where some broadcasters are so badly spoken that they are not only unpleasant to listen to but barely comprehensible.

Whether English is your first or a second language you will find this series not only a delight to the ear and the mind but also a reliable guide to good Standard English pronunciation. And having the text of the recordings is also valuable, partly for those needing help with spelling and the written language generally but mainly so that students of good English can read the text aloud themselves to copy and practise what they have heard. Even very young children will benefit from listening to their favourite stories and rhymes, either from our recordings or from your reading the text to them.

To keep abreast of the new titles in our series we warmly invite you to visit our website and register your interest in receiving our newsletters. You will also find full details of the new, all-on-film *English Speech and Pronunciation* course, every word of which is presented on twenty hours of superb video by top actors and tutors. There is nothing like this in the world. It is completely new, totally absorbing and highly effective. You can receive it either as a download to your computer or tablet or other suitable device, or as a boxed set of course book and 14 DVDs. So many overseas students learning English cannot know if their tutors speak well or not. With this course they can be certain that they are hearing the best, clearest, most universally comprehensible and most widely admired English speech and pronunciation not only in the United Kingdom but through the world (even in America, where they love and often envy the classic English accent!). This new *Educated English* series also serves as an enjoyable and valuable form of continuing education for students of the *English Speech and Pronunciation* course.

But do have a look for yourself at all we can offer by visiting our website, where you will be able to see an overview and samples from the course, browse in our online shop, register to receive our online newsletters, and enjoy the blogs which expose the silly solecisms of speech and pronunciation to which we are daily subjected, not least from those who should know better! We are also always glad to hear from you and have your comments and suggestions. We do hope you will enjoy this first title in the *Educated English* series and that you will join the battle to restore good English speech and pronunciation to its proper place in a civilised world.

www.speechandpronunciation.com

Macaulay, *The Lays* and *Horatius*

Some of the world's finest, most memorable and gripping poetry is epic. It is full of action, and the hearer or reader (and it is best read out loud) is carried along by the pace of the story and the rhythm of the verse.

Epic poetry is often at its best when it looks back to a heroic age and tells mythical or semi-mythical stories. Perhaps the greatest of all epics, at least in western literature, are the oldest, Homer's colossal Greek epics the *Iliad* and the *Odyssey*. Composed orally in the so-called Dark Ages that followed the collapse of the great Bronze Age or Mycenaean Greek civilisation and when the art of writing had been lost for at least three centuries, the *Iliad* is perhaps the greatest war story and the *Odyssey* the greatest adventure story ever.

The Romans, the conquerors of Greece who were themselves captivated by Greek civilisation and literature, tried to copy these great epics. Virgil in particular made a good job of his *Aeneid*, the story of the Trojan prince Aeneas who survived the destruction of Troy by the Greeks in the Trojan War, and was led by divine guidance to Italy, where he was found a role, somewhat artificially, in the foundation myths of Rome. But good as it is, the *Aeneid* sounds artificial and derivative compared with Homer's oral epics. Although it is a rattling good story, the verse is good, and it carries the reader along at a good pace, it reeks of the study rather than the camp fire or the banqueting hall with the goblets of wine circulating and the well-fed company ready for a bard to entertain them. To be perfectly frank (and dangerously irreverent!), when it comes to epic poetry based on the semi-mythical history of early Rome, I prefer the Victorian English ballads, and pre-eminently Lord Macaulay's *Lays of Ancient Rome*.

These days of ill-educated politicians, or politicians who feel they are being undemocratic if they do not disguise or belittle their education, make us long for a return to those now almost unbelievable days when our political leaders were cultivated, and the electorate not only admired them for it but expected it of them. The greatest of our Victorian Prime Ministers, Gladstone and Disraeli, were both men of a depth and breadth of education and culture that are unimaginable in almost all of today's pathetic bunch of second-raters. Gladstone, steeped in the Classics, read Homer in the original Greek, and among his significant literary output were books and articles on the Homeric epics and their composition. Disraeli wrote historical novels. And they were not unusual among politicians. One of the greatest and most humane and fair-minded of Victorian ministers was Thomas Babbington Macaulay, who later became Baron Macaulay, and was one of the members of the House of Lords who really deserved his ennoblement.

When he first became a Member of Parliament his maiden speech was a brilliantly worded plea for the removal of the political and social disabilities of the Jews, and he followed this up with a series of major speeches on parliamentary reform that culminated in the Great Reform Act of 1832 that made the electoral system far more representative and democratic. Then in 1834, after the Government of India Act had taken control of the Indian empire from the East India Company, he went to India, served on the Governor's Council, and was responsible for far-reaching educational reforms. Most importantly he persuaded the Governor to make English the medium of instruction in higher education, from the sixth year onwards, in place of Sanskrit or Persian.

His aim was to "educate a people who cannot at present be educated by means of their mother tongue" and thus, by incorporating English, he also sought to enrich the Indian languages in order that "they could become vehicles for European scientific, historical, and literary expression". He had enormous respect for Indian civilisation, and when we now see the wonderful growth of a free and independent India as one of the world's most important countries and its largest democracy, we understand his vision for fusing these two great cultures, and also the reverence that India pays to his memory – not least among the Dalits, formerly and horribly called "Untouchables", who regard English as one of the main avenues through which they can rise in what is still (in practice if not in theory) a caste-based society that traditionally confined them to the nastiest and dirtiest of menial jobs. And Macaulay was as great and beneficent a contributor to India in the field of law as in that of education. He drafted the India Penal Code of 1860, which was then adopted in many of the empire's colonies and is still the basis of their legal systems today, so many years after their independence.

His was an incredibly busy and useful life, yet this supremely civilised and cultivated man found time to write some first-rate and hugely popular epic poetry in English – not on the scale of Milton's magnificent epics *Paradise Lost* and *Paradise Regained*, yet perhaps more immediately attractive to today's readers and as a stepping stone to the great Milton and the like. Macaulay's *Lays of Ancient Rome* are glorious, rolling poetry with tremendous pace and rhythm. They are both exciting and moving, and no man should feel unmanly to find himself with a moist eye when hearing or reading some of the passages, many of which are truly memorable and eminently quotable.

Macaulay died before he was sixty, and was sadly too ill to take up the seat in the House of Lords in which who knows what further good he could have done. But his legacy is still with us, not only in the United Kingdom but in many countries of the Commonwealth of Nations; and not least among the inheritance we enjoy from him are his ballads – *The Lays of Ancient Rome.*

Before you hear the first of them, *Horatius*, perhaps it would be useful to set the scene. All states have their creation myths, and their early "history" owes more to traditional stories, legends and imagination than to fact. Long before Aeneas was introduced to the foundation story by Virgil, tradition had it that Rome was founded by two brothers from the ancient Latin city of Alba Longa. Their names were Romulus and Remus. A usurping king had tried to destroy them when they were born by throwing them into the River Tiber in a crate; but divine providence brought them safely to land, where they were suckled by a she-wolf before being found by the royal shepherd and his wife, who brought them up. I shall not go into the whole story, though it's a good one. Suffice it to say that this is what is meant when the three heroic Romans defending the bridge are referred to as "the she-wolf's litter".

Rome started life as one of many little Latin city-states, if that is not too grand a name for what was originally a hill-top village of shepherds and their families. For several generations it was ruled by a series of kings, some of them, including the last one, Etruscan. The Etruscans were not Latins. They spoke their own mysterious language, Etruscan, which was not Indo-European at all and still largely defies translation because so few of its inscriptions remain. They seem to have been a civilised people, though they are known to us sadly only by what the Romans said about them and through archaeology, particularly their elegantly painted tombs, which depict what must have been a pleasant society (at least for those on the top of it). One of their chief cities was called Tarquinii, and at the time of the events chronicled in *Horatius* the leading one seems to have been Clusium. The Etruscans inhabited more or less what is now known as Tuscany (the ancient Etruria), in a loose confederation of city-states.

We are nearing the end of the sixth century B.C. Rome has recently revolted against its last king, the Etruscan monarch Tarquinius Superbus – Tarquin the Proud. The King's son, "false Sextus", had raped a distinguished Roman lady called Lucretia, who told her husband and then committed suicide. This was the "deed of shame" referred to in the ballads, and it sparked a revolution, led by Junius Brutus. His movement not only expelled the Etruscan dynasty and its supporters but abolished monarchy altogether and established an aristocratic republic. Henceforth the executive power would be in the hands of two annually elected Consuls, advised by the Senate or "Fathers" of Rome, and there also seems to have been a democratic element to the constitution, albeit a rather embryonic one. And when Julius Caesar was attempting to destroy the republic and make himself monarch some four and a half centuries later, it was a descendant and namesake of this Brutus who was one of his leading assassins on the Ides of March, B.C. 44.

Macaulay does not fail to include some valuable political observations that are as true now as they were in the declining days of the Roman Republic, ultimately destroyed by Caesar and his heirs, despite the efforts of Brutus, Cassius and the die-hard republicans. When we look at the politics of our decaying democracies we too can long for "the brave days of old", when "none was for a party" and "all were for the state"; for even if there never was such a golden age, there have been great crises in the history of all nations when there was a better balance between party politics and the common good than there is today.

But we'd better start at the beginning. The Tarquins were not going to accept their expulsion without a fight. "False Sextus", son and heir of the ousted Tarquinius Superbus, appealed to Lars Porsena, king of one of the greatest of the Etruscan cities, to reinstate him by force. This mighty monarch summoned overwhelming forces from all the cities of the Etruscan confederation, and together they marched on Rome.

Now listen to what happened ...

HORATIUS

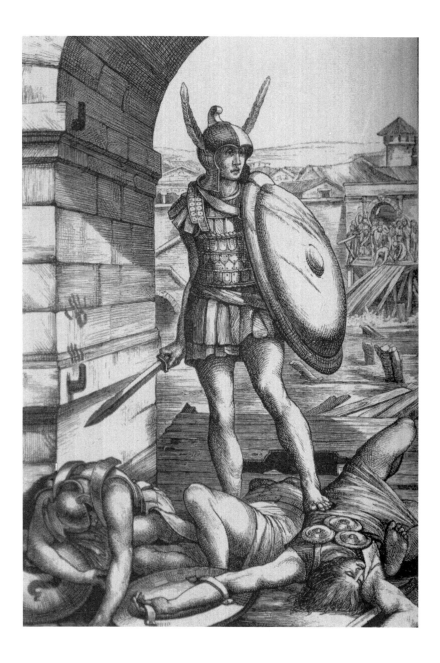

I

Lars Porsena of Clusium
        By the Nine Gods he swore
That the great house of Tarquin
        Should suffer wrong no more.
By the Nine Gods he swore it,
        And named a trysting day,
And bade his messengers ride forth,
East and west and south and north,
        To summon his array.

II

East and west and south and north
        The messengers ride fast,
And tower and town and cottage
        Have heard the trumpet's blast.
Shame on the false Etruscan
        Who lingers in his home,
When Porsena of Clusium
        Is on the march for Rome.

III

The horsemen and the footmen
        Are pouring in amain
From many a stately market-place;
        From many a fruitful plain;
From many a lonely hamlet,
        Which, hid by beech and pine,
Like an eagle's nest, hangs on the crest
        Of purple Apennine;

IV

From lordly Volaterræ,
    Where scowls the far-famed hold
Piled by the hands of giants
    For godlike kings of old;
From seagirt Populonia,
    Whose sentinels descry
Sardinia's snowy mountain-tops
    Fringing the southern sky;

V

From the proud mart of Pisæ,
    Queen of the western waves,
Where ride Massilia's triremes
    Heavy with fair-haired slaves;
From where sweet Clanis wanders
    Through corn and vines and flowers;
From where Cortona lifts to heaven
    Her diadem of towers.

VI

Tall are the oaks whose acorns
    Drop in dark Auser's rill;
Fat are the stags that champ the boughs
    Of the Ciminian hill;
Beyond all streams Clitumnus
    Is to the herdsman dear;
Best of all pools the fowler loves
    The great Volsinian mere.

VII

But now no stroke of woodman
    Is heard by Auser's rill;
No hunter tracks the stag's green path
    Up the Ciminian hill;
Unwatched along Clitumnus
    Grazes the milk-white steer;
Unharmed the water fowl may dip
    In the Volsinian mere.

VIII

The harvests of Arretium,
    This year, old men shall reap;
This year, young boys in Umbro
    Shall plunge the struggling sheep;
And in the vats of Luna,
    This year, the must shall foam
Round the white feet of laughing girls
    Whose sires have marched to Rome.

IX

There be thirty chosen prophets,
    The wisest of the land,
Who alway by Lars Porsena
    Both morn and evening stand:
Evening and morn the Thirty
    Have turned the verses o'er,
Traced from the right on linen white
    By mighty seers of yore.

X

And with one voice the Thirty
    Have their glad answer given:
"Go forth, go forth, Lars Porsena;
    Go forth, beloved of Heaven;
Go, and return in glory
    To Clusium's royal dome;
And hang round Nurscia's altars
    The golden shields of Rome."

XI

And now hath every city
    Sent up her tale of men;
The foot are fourscore thousand,
    The horse are thousands ten.
Before the gates of Sutrium
    Is met the great array.
A proud man was Lars Porsena
    Upon the trysting day.

XII

For all the Etruscan armies
    Were ranged beneath his eye,
And many a banished Roman,
    And many a stout ally;
And with a mighty following
    To join the muster came
The Tusculan Mamilius,
    Prince of the Latin name.

XIII

But by the yellow Tiber
    Was tumult and affright:
From all the spacious champaign
    To Rome men took their flight.
A mile around the city,
    The throng stopped up the ways;
A fearful sight it was to see
    Through two long nights and days.

XIV

For aged folks on crutches,
    And women great with child,
And mothers sobbing over babes
    That clung to them and smiled,
And sick men borne in litters
    High on the necks of slaves,
And troops of sun-burned husbandmen
    With reaping-hooks and staves,

XV

And droves of mules and asses
    Laden with skins of wine,
And endless flocks of goats and sheep,
    And endless herds of kine,
And endless trains of wagons
    That creaked beneath the weight
Of corn-sacks and of household goods,
    Choked every roaring gate.

XVI

Now, from the rock Tarpeian,
    Could the wan burghers spy
The line of blazing villages
    Red in the midnight sky.
The Fathers of the City,
    They sat all night and day,
For every hour some horseman came
    With tidings of dismay.

XVII

To eastward and to westward
    Have spread the Tuscan bands;
Nor house, nor fence, nor dovecote
    In Crustumerium stands.
Verbenna down to Ostia
    Hath wasted all the plain;
Astur hath stormed Janiculum,
    And the stout guards are slain.

XVIII

I wis, in all the Senate,
    There was no heart so bold,
But sore it ached, and fast it beat,
    When that ill news was told.
Forthwith up rose the Consul,
    Up rose the Fathers all;
In haste they girded up their gowns,
    And hied them to the wall.

XIX

They held a council standing,
    Before the River-Gate;
Short time was there, ye well may guess,
    For musing or debate.
Out spake the Consul roundly:
    "The bridge must straight go down;
For, since Janiculum is lost,
    Nought else can save the town."

XX

Just then a scout came flying,
    All wild with haste and fear;
"To arms! to arms! Sir Consul:
    Lars Porsena is here."
On the low hills to westward
    The Consul fixed his eye,
And saw the swarthy storm of dust
    Rise fast along the sky.

XXI

And nearer fast and nearer
    Doth the red whirlwind come;
And louder still and still more loud,
From underneath that rolling cloud,
Is heard the trumpet's war-note proud,
    The trampling, and the hum.
And plainly and more plainly
    Now through the gloom appears,
Far to left and far to right,
In broken gleams of dark-blue light,
The long array of helmets bright,
    The long array of spears.

XXII

And plainly and more plainly,
 Above that glimmering line,
Now might ye see the banners
 Of twelve fair cities shine;
But the banner of proud Clusium
 Was highest of them all,
The terror of the Umbrian,
 The terror of the Gaul.

XXIII

And plainly and more plainly
 Now might the burghers know,
By port and vest, by horse and crest,
 Each warlike Lucumo.
There Cilnius of Arretium
 On his fleet roan was seen;
And Astur of the four-fold shield,
Girt with the brand none else may wield,
Tolumnius with the belt of gold,
And dark Verbenna from the hold
 By reedy Thrasymene.

XXIV

Fast by the royal standard,
 O'erlooking all the war,
Lars Porsena of Clusium
 Sat in his ivory car.
By the right wheel rode Mamilius,
 Prince of the Latian name;
And by the left false Sextus,
 That wrought the deed of shame.

XXV

But when the face of Sextus
    Was seen among the foes,
A yell that rent the firmament
    From all the town arose.
On the house-tops was no woman
    But spat towards him and hissed,
No child but screamed out curses,
    And shook its little fist.

XXVI

But the Consul's brow was sad,
    And the Consul's speech was low,
And darkly looked he at the wall,
    And darkly at the foe.
"Their van will be upon us
    Before the bridge goes down;
And if they once may win the bridge,
    What hope to save the town?"

XXVII

Then out spake brave Horatius,
    The Captain of the Gate:
"To every man upon this earth
    Death cometh soon or late.
And how can man die better
    Than facing fearful odds,
For the ashes of his fathers,
    And the temples of his Gods,

XXVIII

"And for the tender mother
    Who dandled him to rest,
And for the wife who nurses
    His baby at her breast,
And for the holy maidens
    Who feed the eternal flame,
To save them from false Sextus
    That wrought the deed of shame?

XXIX

"Haul down the bridge, Sir Consul,
    With all the speed ye may;
I, with two more to help me,
    Will hold the foe in play.
In yon strait path a thousand
    May well be stopped by three.
Now who will stand on either hand,
    And keep the bridge with me?"

XXX

Then out spake Spurius Lartius;
    A Ramnian proud was he:
"Lo, I will stand at thy right hand,
    And keep the bridge with thee."
And out spake strong Herminius;
    Of Titian blood was he:
"I will abide on thy left side,
    And keep the bridge with thee."

XXXI

"Horatius," quoth the Consul,
    "As thou sayest, so let it be."
And straight against that great array
    Forth went the dauntless Three.
For Romans in Rome's quarrel
    Spared neither land nor gold,
Nor son nor wife, nor limb nor life,
    In the brave days of old.

XXXII

Then none was for a party;
    Then all were for the state;
Then the great man helped the poor,
    And the poor man loved the great:
Then lands were fairly portioned;
    Then spoils were fairly sold:
The Romans were like brothers
    In the brave days of old.

XXXIII

Now Roman is to Roman
    More hateful than a foe,
And the Tribunes beard the high,
    And the Fathers grind the low.
As we wax hot in faction,
    In battle we wax cold:
Wherefore men fight not as they fought
    In the brave days of old.

XXXIV

Now while the Three were tightening
   Their harness on their backs,
The Consul was the foremost man
   To take in hand an axe:
And Fathers mixed with Commons
   Seized hatchet, bar, and crow,
And smote upon the planks above,
   And loosed the props below.

XXXV

Meanwhile the Tuscan army,
   Right glorious to behold,
Came flashing back the noonday light,
Rank behind rank, like surges bright
   Of a broad sea of gold.
Four hundred trumpets sounded
   A peal of warlike glee,
As that great host, with measured tread,
And spears advanced, and ensigns spread,
Rolled slowly towards the bridge's head,
   Where stood the dauntless Three.

XXXVI

The Three stood calm and silent,
   And looked upon the foes,
And a great shout of laughter
   From all the vanguard rose:
And forth three chiefs came spurring
   Before that deep array;
To earth they sprang, their swords they drew,
And lifted high their shields, and flew
   To win the narrrow way;

XXXVII

Aunus from green Tifernum,
  Lord of the Hill of Vines;
And Seius, whose eight hundred slaves
  Sicken in Ilva's mines;
And Picus, long to Clusium
  Vassal in peace and war,
Who led to fight his Umbrian powers
From that grey crag where, girt with towers,
The fortress of Nequinum lowers
  O'er the pale waves of Nar.

XXXVIII

Stout Lartius hurled down Aunus
   Into the stream beneath;
Herminius struck at Seius,
   And clove him to the teeth;
At Picus brave Horatius
   Darted one fiery thrust;
And the proud Umbrian's gilded arms
   Clashed in the bloody dust.

XXXIX

Then Ocnus of Falerii
   Rushed on the Roman Three;
And Lausulus of Urgo,
   The rover of the sea;
And Aruns of Volsinium,
   Who slew the great wild boar,
The great wild boar that had his den
Amidst the reeds of Cosa's fen,
And wasted fields, and slaughtered men,
   Along Albinia's shore.

XL

Herminius smote down Aruns:
   Lartius laid Ocnus low:
Right to the heart of Lausulus
   Horatius sent a blow.
"Lie there," he cried, "fell pirate!
   No more, aghast and pale,
From Ostia's walls the crowd shall mark
The track of thy destroying bark.
No more Campania's hinds shall fly
To woods and caverns when they spy
   Thy thrice accursed sail."

XLI

But now no sound of laughter
    Was heard among the foes.
A wild and wrathful clamour
    From all the vanguard rose.
Six spears' lengths from the entrance
    Halted that deep array,
And for a space no man came forth
    To win the narrow way.

XLII

But hark! the cry is Astur:
    And lo! the ranks divide;
And the great Lord of Luna
    Comes with his stately stride.
Upon his ample shoulders
    Clangs loud the four-fold shield,
And in his hand he shakes the brand
    Which none but he can wield.

XLIII

He smiled on those bold Romans
    A smile serene and high;
He eyed the flinching Tuscans,
    And scorn was in his eye.
Quoth he, "The she-wolf's litter
    Stand savagely at bay:
But will ye dare to follow,
    If Astur clears the way?"

XLIV

Then, whirling up his broadsword
  With both hands to the height,
He rushed against Horatius,
  And smote with all his might.
With shield and blade Horatius
  Right deftly turned the blow.
The blow, though turned, came yet too nigh;
It missed his helm, but gashed his thigh:
The Tuscans raised a joyful cry
  To see the red blood flow.

XLV

He reeled, and on Herminius
  He leaned one breathing-space;
Then, like a wild cat mad with wounds,
  Sprang right at Astur's face.
Through teeth, and skull, and helmet
  So fierce a thrust he sped,
The good sword stood a hand-breadth out
  Behind the Tuscan's head.

XLVI

And the great Lord of Luna
  Fell at that deadly stroke,
As falls on Mount Alvernus
  A thunder-smitten oak:
Far o'er the crashing forest
  The giant arms lie spread;
And the pale augurs, muttering low,
  Gaze on the blasted head.

XLVII

On Astur's throat Horatius
Right firmly pressed his heel,
And thrice and four times tugged amain,
Ere he wrenched out the steel.
"And see," he cried, "the welcome,
Fair guests, that waits you here!
What noble Lucomo comes next
To taste our Roman cheer?"

XLVIII

But at his haughty challenge
A sullen murmur ran,
Mingled of wrath, and shame, and dread,
Along that glittering van.
There lacked not men of prowess,
Nor men of lordly race;
For all Etruria's noblest
Were round the fatal place.

XLIX

But all Etruria's noblest
Felt their hearts sink to see
On the earth the bloody corpses,
In the path the dauntless Three:
And, from the ghastly entrance
Where those bold Romans stood,
All shrank, like boys who unaware,
Ranging the woods to start a hare,
Come to the mouth of the dark lair
Where, growling low, a fierce old bear
Lies amidst bones and blood.

L

Was none who would be foremost
    To lead such dire attack;
But those behind cried, "Forward!"
    And those before cried, "Back!"
And backward now and forward
    Wavers the deep array;
And on the tossing sea of steel
To and fro the standards reel;
And the victorious trumpet-peal
    Dies fitfully away.

LI

Yet one man for one moment
    Strode out before the crowd;
Well known was he to all the Three,
    And they gave him greeting loud.
"Now welcome, welcome, Sextus!
    Now welcome to thy home!
Why dost thou stay, and turn away?
    Here lies the road to Rome."

LII

Thrice looked he at the city;
    Thrice looked he at the dead;
And thrice came on in fury,
    And thrice turned back in dread:
And, white with fear and hatred,
    Scowled at the narrow way
Where, wallowing in a pool of blood,
    The bravest Tuscans lay.

LIII

But meanwhile axe and lever
    Have manfully been plied;
And now the bridge hangs tottering
    Above the boiling tide.
"Come back, come back, Horatius!"
    Loud cried the Fathers all.
"Back, Lartius! back, Herminius!
    Back, ere the ruin fall!"

LIV

Back darted Spurius Lartius;
    Herminius darted back:
And, as they passed, beneath their feet
    They felt the timbers crack.
But when they turned their faces,
    And on the farther shore
Saw brave Horatius stand alone,
    They would have crossed once more.

LV

But with a crash like thunder
    Fell every loosened beam,
And, like a dam, the mighty wreck
    Lay right athwart the stream:
And a long shout of triumph
    Rose from the walls of Rome,
As to the highest turret-tops
    Was splashed the yellow foam.

LVI

And, like a horse unbroken
  When first he feels the rein,
The furious river struggled hard,
  And tossed his tawny mane,
And burst the curb and bounded,
  Rejoicing to be free,
And whirling down, in fierce career,
Battlement, and plank, and pier,
  Rushed headlong to the sea.

LVII

Alone stood brave Horatius,
  But constant still in mind;
Thrice thirty thousand foes before,
  And the broad flood behind.
"Down with him!" cried false Sextus,
  With a smile on his pale face.
"Now yield thee," cried Lars Porsena,
  "Now yield thee to our grace."

LVIII

Round turned he, as not deigning
  Those craven ranks to see;
Nought spake he to Lars Porsena,
  To Sextus nought spake he;
But he saw on Palatinus
  The white porch of his home;
And he spake to the noble river
  That rolls by the towers of Rome.

LIX

"Oh, Tiber! Father Tiber!
    To whom the Romans pray,
A Roman's life, a Roman's arms,
    Take thou in charge this day!"
So he spake, and speaking sheathed
    The good sword by his side,
And with his harness on his back,
    Plunged headlong in the tide.

LX

No sound of joy or sorrow
    Was heard from either bank;
But friends and foes in dumb surprise,
With parted lips and straining eyes,
    Stood gazing where he sank;
And when above the surges,
    They saw his crest appear,
All Rome sent forth a rapturous cry,
And even the ranks of Tuscany
    Could scarce forbear to cheer.

LXI

But fiercely ran the current,
    Swollen high by months of rain:
And fast his blood was flowing;
    And he was sore in pain,
And heavy with his armour,
    And spent with changing blows:
And oft they thought him sinking,
    But still again he rose.

LXII

Never, I ween, did swimmer,
  In such an evil case,
Struggle through such a raging flood
  Safe to the landing place:
But his limbs were borne up bravely
  By the brave heart within,
And our good father Tiber
  Bare bravely up his chin.

LXIII

"Curse on him!" quoth false Sextus;
  "Will not the villain drown?
But for this stay, ere close of day
  We should have sacked the town!"
"Heaven help him!" quoth Lars Porsena
  "And bring him safe to shore;
For such a gallant feat of arms
  Was never seen before."

LXIV

And now he feels the bottom;
  Now on dry earth he stands;
Now round him throng the Fathers;
  To press his gory hands;
And now, with shouts and clapping,
  And noise of weeping loud,
He enters through the River-Gate
  Borne by the joyous crowd.

LXV

They gave him of the corn-land,
  That was of public right,
As much as two strong oxen
  Could plough from morn till night;
And they made a molten image,
  And set it up on high,
And there it stands unto this day
  To witness if I lie.

LXVI

It stands in the Comitium
  Plain for all folk to see;
Horatius in his harness,
  Halting upon one knee:
And underneath is written,
  In letters all of gold,
How valiantly he kept the bridge
  In the brave days of old.

LXVII

And still his name sounds stirring
  Unto the men of Rome,
As the trumpet-blast that cries to them
  To charge the Volscian home;
And wives still pray to Juno
  For boys with hearts as bold
As his who kept the bridge so well
  In the brave days of old.

LXVIII

And in the nights of winter,
  When the cold north winds blow,
And the long howling of the wolves
  Is heard amidst the snow;
When round the lonely cottage
  Roars loud the tempest's din,
And the good logs of Algidus
  Roar louder yet within;

LXIX

When the oldest cask is opened,
  And the largest lamp is lit;
When the chestnuts glow in the embers,
  And the kid turns on the spit;
When young and old in circle
  Around the firebrands close;
When the girls are weaving baskets,
  And the lads are shaping bows;

LXX

When the goodman mends his armour,
  And trims his helmet's plume;
When the goodwife's shuttle merrily
  Goes flashing through the loom;
With weeping and with laughter
  Still is the story told,
How well Horatius kept the bridge
  In the brave days of old.

Rome's second fight for survival

Thanks to Horatius and his dauntless colleagues the infant Republic survived this attempt to stifle her growth, but she would have to face many more life-or-death struggles with powerful local enemies before she grew strong enough to start taking them on in her turn as a preliminary to conquering the whole of Italy and then creating the greatest empire of the ancient western world.

After failing to get himself reinstated by Lars Porsena of Clusium, the vengeful Sextus and his aged father, Tarquinius the Proud, took refuge with his son-on-law, Mamilius Octavius of Tusculum. This was not an Etruscan but a Latin city, and when Mamilius agreed to bring together a confederation of Latin cities against Rome, he and his fellow Latins were no doubt glad of the excuse to bring to heel an arrogant upstart state that had expelled its monarchy and seemed to be flexing its muscles among its neighbours. Giving the Romans a good drubbing and reinstalling the vengeful Etruscan dynasty would usefully put the lid on any territorial ambitions the new government might have.

Like the earlier invasion by the Etruscans, this expedition by an alliance of Latin states was numerically overwhelming, and this time the Romans were saved by divine aid as well as their own courage. The Romans did not wait to defend their city but marched out in full force to meet their enemies in the field at the Battle of Lake Regillus. It was a struggle for survival, and in so grave a crisis they decided to suspend the constitution and appoint a single army commander and head of state (rather than the two Consuls, who normally commanded the army in turn). They called this supremo the Dictator, his appointment was for a maximum of six months, and he was allowed to appoint a second in command called the Master of the Horse. Thus, innocuously, came into the language and into politics a word and a role that have since become anathema to believers in democracy, which it has done its best to destroy.

Macaulay begins this ballad with a great religious festival and parade at Rome commemorating this great deliverance on the Ides of Quintilis (the 15th of July by our reckoning) some two hundred years later. It was the feast day of the divine Dioscuri, the twin heroes Castor and Pollux, whom we still see in the night sky as the two brightest stars in the constellation Gemini ("The Twins"). Their cult most probably had its origins in warlike Sparta, called Lacedaemon in the ballad, but it became popular all over the Greco-Roman world, and had no doubt come to Italy through the many Greek maritime colonies established there from the eighth to the sixth centuries BC.

The "Great Twin Brethren" as Macaulay calls them are generally depicted in art as young knights on horseback, and they were known to appear and lend their aid when the brave whom they loved, and who loved them, and who were fighting for the right, were in great danger. Rome was seldom in greater danger than in the Battle of Regillus, and thanks to Macaulay we can still join the crowds at the great festival to watch the procession of knights and hear a bard tell the story of what happened on that fateful day, not long after the defence of the bridge by Horatius and his two friends, one of whom, Herminius, is a great hero in this struggle too …

THE BATTLE OF LAKE REGILLUS

I

Ho, trumpets, sound a war-note!
    Ho, lictors, clear the way!
The Knights will ride, in all their pride,
    Along the streets to-day.
To-day the doors and windows
    Are hung with garlands all,
From Castor in the Forum,
    To Mars without the wall.
Each Knight is robed in purple,
    With olive each is crowned;
A gallant war-horse under each
    Paws haughtily the ground.
While flows the Yellow River,
    While stands the Sacred Hill,
The proud Ides of Quintilis
    Shall have such honour still.
Gay are the Martian Kalends,
    December's Nones are gay,
But the proud Ides, when the squadron rides,
    Shall be Rome's whitest day.

II

Unto the Great Twin Brethren
    We keep this solemn feast.
Swift, swift, the Great Twin Brethren
    Came spurring from the east.
They came o'er wild Parthenius
    Tossing in waves of pine,
O'er Cirrha's dome, o'er Adria's foam,
    O'er purple Apennine,
From where with flutes and dances
    Their ancient mansion rings,
In lordly Lacedæmon,
    The City of two kings,
To where, by Lake Regillus,
    Under the Porcian height,
All in the lands of Tusculum,
    Was fought the glorious fight.

III

Now on the place of slaughter
    Are cots and sheepfolds seen
And rows of vines, and fields of wheat,
    And apple-orchards green;
The swine crush the big acorns
    That fall from Corne's oaks.
Upon the turf by the Fair Fount
    The reaper's pottage smokes.
The fisher baits his angle;
    The hunter twangs his bow;
Little they think on those strong limbs
    That moulder deep below.
Little they think how sternly
    That day the trumpets pealed;
How in the slippery swamp of blood
    Warrior and war-horse reeled;
How wolves came with fierce gallop,
    And crows on eager wings,
To tear the flesh of captains,
    And peck the eyes of kings;
How thick the dead lay scattered
    Under the Porcian height;
How through the gates of Tusculum
    Raved the wild stream of flight;
And how the Lake Regillus
    Bubbled with crimson foam,
What time the Thirty Cities
    Came forth to war with Rome.

IV

But, Roman, when thou standest
Upon that holy ground,
Look thou with heed on the dark rock
That girds the dark lake round.
So shalt thou see a hoof-mark
Stamped deep into the flint:
It was not hoof of mortal steed
That made so strange a dint:
There to the Great Twin Brethren
Vow thou thy vows, and pray
That they, in tempest and in fight,
Will keep thy head alway.

V

Since last the Great Twin Brethren
Of mortal eyes were seen,
Have years gone by an hundred
And fourscore and thirteen.
That summer a Virginius
Was Consul first in place;
The second was stout Aulus,
Of the Posthumian race.
The Herald of the Latines
From Gabii came in state:
The Herald of the Latines
Passed through Rome's Eastern Gate:
The Herald of the Latines
Did in our Forum stand;
And there he did his office,
A sceptre in his hand.

VI

"Hear, Senators and people
          Of the good town of Rome,
The Thirty Cities charge you
          To bring the Tarquins home:
And if ye still be stubborn
          To work the Tarquins wrong,
The Thirty Cities warn you,
          Look your walls be strong."

VII

Then spake the Consul Aulus,
          He spake a bitter jest:
"Once the jay sent a message
          Unto the eagle's nest:–
Now yield thou up thine eyrie
          Unto the carrion-kite,
Or come forth valiantly, and face
          The jays in deadly fight.–
Forth looked in wrath the eagle;
          And carrion-kite and jay,
Soon as they saw his beak and claw,
          Fled screaming far away."

VIII

The Herald of the Latines
    Hath hied him back in state;
The Fathers of the City
    Are met in high debate.
Then spake the elder Consul,
    An ancient man and wise:
"Now harken, Conscript Fathers,
    To that which I advise.
In seasons of great peril
    'Tis good that one bear sway;
Then choose we a Dictator,
    Whom all men shall obey.
Camerium knows how deeply
    The sword of Aulus bites,
And all our city calls him
    The man of seventy fights.
Then let him be Dictator
    For six months and no more,
And have a Master of the Knights,
    And axes twenty-four."

IX

So Aulus was Dictator,
    The man of seventy fights;
He made Æbutius Elva
    His Master of the Knights.
On the third morn thereafter,
    At dawning of the day,
Did Aulus and Æbutius
    Set forth with their array.
Sempronius Atratinus
    Was left in charge at home
With boys, and with grey-headed men,
    To keep the walls of Rome.
Hard by the Lake Regillus
    Our camp was pitched at night;
Eastward a mile the Latines lay,
    Under the Porcian height.
Far over hill and valley
    Their mighty host was spread;
And with their thousand watch-fires
    The midnight sky was red.

X

Up rose the golden morning
    Over the Porcian height,
The proud Ides of Quintilis
    Marked evermore in white.
Not without secret trouble
    Our bravest saw the foe;
For girt by threescore thousand spears,
    The thirty standards rose.
From every warlike city
    That boasts the Latian name,
Foredoomed to dogs and vultures,
    That gallant army came;
From Setia's purple vineyards,
    From Norba's ancient wall,
From the white streets of Tusculum,
    The proudest town of all;
From where the Witch's Fortress
    O'er hangs the dark-blue seas;
From the still glassy lake that sleeps
    Beneath Aricia's trees –
Those trees in whose dim shadow
    The ghastly priest doth reign,
The priest who slew the slayer,
    And shall himself be slain;
From the drear banks of Ufens,
    Where flights of marsh-fowl play,
And buffaloes lie wallowing
    Through the hot summer's day;

From the gigantic watch-towers,
    No work of earthly men,
Whence Cora's sentinels o'erlook
    The never-ending fen;
From the Laurentian jungle,
    The wild hog's reedy home;
From the green steeps whence Anio leaps
    In floods of snow-white foam.

XI

Aricia, Cora, Norba,
    Velitræ, with the might
Of Setia and of Tusculum,
    Were marshalled on the right:
The leader was Mamilius,
    Prince of the Latian name;
Upon his head a helmet
    Of red gold shone like flame:
High on a gallant charger
    Of dark-grey hue he rode;
Over his gilded armour
    A vest of purple flowed,
Woven in the land of sunrise
    By Syria's dark-browed daughters,
And by the sails of Carthage brought
    Far o'er the southern waters.

XII

Lavinium and Laurentum
    Had on the left their post,
With all the banners of the marsh,
    And banners of the coast.
Their leader was false Sextus,
    That wrought the deed of shame:
With restless pace and haggard face
    To his last field he came.
Men said he saw strange visions
    Which none beside might see;
And that strange sounds were in his ears
    Which none might hear but he.
A woman fair and stately,
    But pale as are the dead,
Oft through the watches of the night
    Sat spinning by his bed.
And as she plied the distaff,
    In a sweet voice and low,
She sang of great old houses,
    And fights fought long ago.
So spun she, and so sang she,
    Until the east was grey.
Then pointed to her bleeding breast,
    And shrieked, and fled away.

XIII

But in the centre thickest
    Were ranged the shields of foes,
And from the centre loudest
    The cry of battle rose.
There Tibur marched and Pedum
    Beneath proud Tarquin's rule,
And Ferentinum of the rock,
    And Gabii of the pool.
There rode the Volscian succours:
    There, in the dark stern ring,
The Roman exiles gathered close
    Around the ancient king.
Though white as Mount Soracte,
    When winter nights are long,
His beard flowed down o'er mail and belt,
    His heart and hand were strong:
Under his hoary eyebrows
    Still flashed forth quenchless rage:
And, if the lance shook in his gripe,
    'Twas more with hate than age.
Close at his side was Titus
    On an Apulian steed,
Titus, the youngest Tarquin,
    Too good for such a breed.

XIV

Now on each side the leaders
    Gave signal for the charge;
And on each side the footmen
    Strode on with lance and targe;
And on each side the horsemen
    Struck their spurs deep in gore,
And front to front the armies
    Met with a mighty roar:
And under that great battle
    The earth with blood was red;
And, like the Pomptine fog at morn,
    The dust hung overhead;
And louder still and louder
    Rose from the darkened field
The braying of the war-horns,
    The clang of sword and shield,
The rush of squadrons sweeping
    Like whirlwinds o'er the plain,
The shouting of the slayers,
    And screeching of the slain.

XV

False Sextus rode out foremost,
    His look was high and bold;
His corslet was of bison's hide,
    Plated with steel and gold.
As glares the famished eagle
    From the Digentian rock
On a choice lamb that bounds alone
    Before Bandusia's flock,
Herminius glared on Sextus,
    And came with eagle speed,
Herminius on black Auster,
    Brave champion on brave steed;
In his right hand the broadsword
    That kept the bridge so well,
And on his helm the crown he won
    When proud Fidenæ fell.
Woe to the maid whose lover
    Shall cross his path to-day!
False Sextus saw, and trembled,
    And turned, and fled away.
As turns, as flies, the woodman
    In the Calabrian brake,
When through the reeds gleams the round eye
    Of that fell speckled snake;
So turned, so fled, false Sextus,
    And hid him in the rear,
Behind the dark Lavinian ranks,
    Bristling with crest and spear.

XVI

But far to the north Æbutius,
    The Master of the Knights,
Gave Tubero of Norba
    To feed the Porcian kites.
Next under those red horse-hoofs
    Flaccus of Setia lay;
Better had he been pruning
    Among his elms that day.
Mamilius saw the slaughter,
    And tossed his golden crest,
And towards the Master of the Knights
    Through the thick battle pressed.
Æbutius smote Mamilius
    So fiercely on the shield
That the great lord of Tusculum
    Well-nigh rolled on the field.
Mamilius smote Æbutius,
    With a good aim and true,
Just where the neck and shoulder join,
    And pierced him through and through;
And brave Æbutius Elva
    Fell swooning to the ground:
But a thick wall of bucklers
    Encompassed him around.
His clients from the battle
    Bare him some little space,
And filled a helm from the dark lake,
    And bathed his brow and face;
And when at last he opened
    His swimming eyes to light,
Men say, the earliest word he spake
    Was, "Friends, how goes the fight?"

XVII

But meanwhile in the centre
    Great deeds of arms were wrought;
There Aulus the Dictator
    And there Valerius fought.
Aulus with his good broadsword
    A bloody passage cleared
To where, amidst the thickest foes,
    He saw the long white beard.
Flat lighted that good broadsword
    Upon proud Tarquin's head.
He dropped the lance: he dropped the reins:
    He fell as fall the dead.
Down Aulus springs to slay him,
    With eyes like coals of fire;
But faster Titus hath sprung down,
    And hath bestrode his sire.
Latian captains, Roman knights,
    Fast down to earth they spring,
And hand to hand they fight on foot
    Around the ancient king.
First Titus gave tall Cæso
    A death wound in the face;
Tall Cæso was the bravest man
    Of the brave Fabian race:
Aulus slew Rex of Gabii,
    The priest of Juno's shrine;
Valerius smote down Julius,
    Of Rome's great Julian line;
Julius, who left his mansion,
    High on the Velian hill,
And through all turns of weal and woe
    Followed proud Tarquin still.

Now right across proud Tarquin
    A corpse was Julius laid;
And Titus groaned with rage and grief,
    And at Valerius made.
Valerius struck at Titus,
    And lopped off half his crest;
But Titus stabbed Valerius
    A span deep in the breast.
Like a mast snapped by the tempest,
    Valerius reeled and fell.
Ah! woe is me for the good house
    That loves the people well!
Then shouted loud the Latines;
    And with one rush they bore
The struggling Romans backward
    Three lances' length and more:
And up they took proud Tarquin,
    And laid him on a shield,
And four strong yeomen bare him,
    Still senseless, from the field.

XVIII

But fiercer grew the fighting
    Around Valerius dead;
For Titus dragged him by the foot
    And Aulus by the head.
"On, Latines, on!" quoth Titus,
    "See how the rebels fly!"
"Romans, stand firm!" quoth Aulus,
    "And win this fight or die!
They must not give Valerius
    To raven and to kite;
For aye Valerius loathed the wrong,
    And aye upheld the right:
And for your wives and babies
    In the front rank he fell.
Now play the men for the good house
    That loves the people well!"

XIX

Then tenfold round the body
      The roar of battle rose,
Like the roar of a burning forest,
      When a strong north wind blows,
Now backward, and now forward,
      Rocked furiously the fray,
Till none could see Valerius,
      And none wist where he lay.
For shivered arms and ensigns
Were heaped there in a mound,
And corpses stiff, and dying men
      That writhed and gnawed the ground:
And wounded horses kicking,
      And snorting purple foam:
Right well did such a couch befit
      A Consular of Rome.

XX

But north looked the Dictator;
      North looked he long and hard,
And spake to Caius Cossus,
      The Captain of his Guard;
"Caius, of all the Romans
      Thou hast the keenest sight,
Say, what through yonder storm of dust
      Comes from the Latian right?"

XXI

Then answered Caius Cossus:
    "I see an evil sight;
The banner of proud Tusculum
    Comes from the Latian right;
I see the pluméd horsemen;
    And far before the rest
I see the dark-grey charger,
    I see the purple vest;
I see the golden helmet
    That shines far off like flame;
So ever rides Mamilius,
    Prince of the Latian name."

XXII

"Now hearken, Caius Cossus:
    Spring on thy horse's back;
Ride as the wolves of Apennine
    Were all upon thy track;
Haste to our southward battle:
    And never draw thy rein
Until thou find Herminius,
    And bid him come amain."

XXIII

So Aulus spake, and turned him
    Again to that fierce strife;
And Caius Cossus mounted,
    And rode for death and life.
Loud clanged beneath his horse-hoofs
    The helmets of the dead,
And many a curdling pool of blood
    Splashed him heel to head.
So came he far to southward,
    Where fought the Roman host,
Against the banners of the marsh
    And banners of the coast.
Like corn before the sickle
    The stout Lavinians fell,
Beneath the edge of the true sword
    That kept the bridge so well.

XXIV

"Herminius! Aulus greets thee;
    He bids thee come with speed,
To help our central battle,
    For sore is there our need.
There wars the youngest Tarquin,
    And there the Crest of Flame,
The Tusculan Mamilius,
    Prince of the Latian name.
Valerius hath fallen fighting
    In front of our array;
And Aulus of the seventy fields
    Alone upholds the day."

XXV

Herminius beat his bosom:
    But never a word he spake.
He clapped his hand on Auster's mane,
    He gave the reins a shake.
Away, away, went Auster,
    Like an arrow from the bow:
Black Auster was the fleetest steed
    From Aufidus to Po.

XXVI

Right glad were all the Romans
    Who, in that hour of dread,
Against great odds bare up the war
    Around Valerius dead,
When from the south the cheering
    Rose with a mighty swell;
"Herminius comes, Herminius,
    Who kept the bridge so well!"

XXVII

Mamilius spied Herminius,
    And dashed across the way.
"Herminius! I have sought thee
    Through many a bloody day.
One of us two, Herminius,
    Shall never more go home.
I will lay on for Tusculum,
    And thou lay on for Rome!"

XXVIII

All round them paused the battle,
    While met in mortal fray
The Roman and the Tusculan,
    The horses black and grey.
Herminius smote Mamilius
    Through breast-plate and through breast,
And fast flowed out the purple blood
    Over the purple vest.
Mamilius smote Herminius
    Through head-piece and through head,
And side by side those chiefs of pride,
    Together fell down dead.
Down fell they dead together
    In a great lake of gore;
And still stood all who saw them fall
    While men might count a score.

XXIX

Fast, fast, with heels wild spurning,
  The dark-grey charger fled:
He burst through ranks of fighting men,
  He sprang o'er heaps of dead.
His bridle far out-streaming,
  His flanks all blood and foam,
He sought the southern mountains,
  The mountains of his home.
The pass was steep and rugged,
  The wolves they howled and whined;
But he ran like a whirlwind up the pass,
  And he left the wolves behind.
Through many a startled hamlet
  Thundered his flying feet;
He rushed through the gate of Tusculum,
  He rushed up the long white street;
He rushed by tower and temple,
  And paused not from his race
Till he stood before his master's door
  In the stately market-place.
And straightway round him gathered
  A pale and trembling crowd,
And when they knew him, cries of rage
  Brake forth, and wailing loud:
And women rent their tresses
  For their great prince's fall;
And old men girt on their old swords,
  And went to man the wall.

XXX

But, like a graven image,
    Black Auster kept his place,
And ever wistfully he looked
    Into his master's face.
The raven-mane that daily,
    With pats and fond caresses,
The young Herminia washed and combed,
    And twined in even tresses,
And decked with coloured ribbons
    From her own gay attire,
Hung sadly o'er her father's corpse
    In carnage and in mire.
Forth with a shout sprang Titus,
    And seized black Auster's rein.
Then Aulus sware a fearful oath,
    And ran at him amain.
"The furies of thy brother
    With me and mine abide,
If one of your accursed house
    Upon black Auster ride!"
As on an Alpine watch-tower
    From heaven comes down the flame,
Full on the neck of Titus
    The blade of Aulus came:
And out the red blood spouted,
    In a wide arch and tall,
As spouts a fountain in the court
    Of some rich Capuan's hall.
The knees of all the Latines
    Were loosened with dismay,
When dead, on dead Herminius,
    The bravest Tarquin lay.

XXXI

And Aulus the Dictator
Stroked Auster's raven mane,
With heed he looked unto the girths,
With heed unto the rein.
"Now bear me well, black Auster,
Into yon thick array;
And thou and I will have revenge
For thy good lord this day."

XXXII

So spake he; and was buckling
Tighter black Auster's band,
When he was aware of a princely pair
That rode at his right hand.
So like they were, no mortal
Might one from other know:
White as snow their armour was:
Their steeds were white as snow.
Never on earthly anvil
Did such rare armour gleam;
And never did such gallant steeds
Drink of an earthly stream.

XXXIII

And all who saw them trembled,
And pale grew every cheek;
And Aulus the Dictator
Scarce gathered voice to speak.
"Say by what name men call you?
What city is your home?
And wherefore ride ye in such guise
Before the ranks of Rome?"

XXXIV

"By many names men call us;
    In many lands we dwell:
Well Samothracia knows us;
    Cyrene knows us well.
Our house in gay Tarentum
    Is hung each morn with flowers:
High o'er the masts of Syracuse
    Our marble portal towers;
But by the proud Eurotas
    Is our dear native home;
And for the right we come to fight
    Before the ranks of Rome."

XXXV

So answered those strange horsemen,
    And each couched low his spear;
And forthwith all the ranks of Rome
    Were bold, and of good cheer:
And on the thirty armies
    Came wonder and affright,
And Ardea wavered on the left,
    And Cora on the right.
"Rome to the charge!" cried Aulus;
    "The foe begins to yield!
Charge for the hearth of Vesta!
    Charge for the Golden Shield!
Let no man stop to plunder,
    But slay, and slay, and slay;
The gods who live forever
    Are on our side to-day."

XXXVI

Then the fierce trumpet-flourish
From earth to heaven arose,
The kites know well the long stern swell
That bids the Romans close.
Then the good sword of Aulus
Was lifted up to slay:
Then, like a crag down Apennine,
Rushed Auster through the fray.
But under those strange horsemen
Still thicker lay the slain;
And after those strange horses
Black Auster toiled in vain.
Behind them Rome's long battle
Came rolling on the foe,
Ensigns dancing wild above,
Blades all in line below.
So comes the Po in flood-time
Upon the Celtic plain;
So comes the squall, blacker than night,
Upon the Adrian main.
Now, by our Sire Quirinus,
It was a goodly sight
To see the thirty standards
Swept down the tide of flight.
So flies the spray of Adria
When the black squall doth blow
So corn-sheaves in the flood-time
Spin down the whirling Po.
False Sextus to the mountains
Turned first his horse's head;

And fast fled Ferentinum,
　　And fast Lanuvium fled.
The horsemen of Nomentum
　　Spurred hard out of the fray;
The footmen of Velitræ
　　Threw shield and spear away.
And underfoot was trampled,
　　Amidst the mud and gore,
The banner of proud Tusculum,
　　That never stooped before:
And down went Flavius Faustus,
　　Who led his stately ranks
From where the apple blossoms wave
　　On Anio's echoing banks,
And Tullus of Arpinum,
　　Chief of the Volscian aids,
And Metius with the long fair curls,
　　The love of Anxur's maids,
And the white head of Vulso,
　　The great Arician seer,
And Nepos of Laurentum
　　The hunter of the deer;
And in the back false Sextus
　　Felt the good Roman steel,
And wriggling in the dust he died,
　　Like a worm beneath the wheel:
And fliers and pursuers
　　Were mingled in a mass;
And far away the battle
　　Went roaring through the pass.

XXXVII

Sempronius Atratinus
 Sat in the Eastern Gate,
Beside him were three Fathers,
 Each in his chair of state;
Fabius, whose nine stout grandsons
 That day were in the field,
And Manlius, eldest of the Twelve
 Who keep the Golden Shield;
And Sergius, the High Pontiff,
 For wisdom far renowned;
In all Etruria's colleges
 Was no such Pontiff found.
And all around the portal,
 And high above the wall,
Stood a great throng of people,
 But sad and silent all;
Young lads and stooping elders
 That might not bear the mail,
Matrons with lips that quivered,
 And maids with faces pale.
Since the first gleam of daylight,
 Sempronius had not ceased
To listen for the rushing
 Of horse-hoofs from the east.
The mist of eve was rising,
 The sun was hastening down,
When he was aware of a princely pair
 Fast pricking towards the town.
So like they were, man never
 Saw twins so like before;
Red with gore their armour was,
 Their steeds were red with gore.

XXXVIII

"Hail to the great Asylum!
Hail to the hill-tops seven!
Hail to the fire that burns for aye,
    And the shield that fell from heaven!
This day, by Lake Regillus,
    Under the Porcian height,
All in the lands of Tusculum
    Was fought a glorious fight.
Tomorrow your Dictator
    Shall bring in triumph home
The spoils of thirty cities
    To deck the shrines of Rome!"

XXXIX

Then burst from that great concourse
        A shout that shook the towers,
And some ran north, and some ran south,
        Crying,"The day is ours!"
But on rode these strange horsemen,
        With slow and lordly pace;
And none who saw their bearing
        Durst ask their name or race.
On rode they to the Forum,
        While laurel-boughs and flowers,
From house-tops and from windows,
        Fell on their crests in showers.
When they drew nigh to Vesta,
        They vaulted down amain,
And washed their horses in the well
        That springs by Vesta's fane.
And straight again they mounted,
        And rode to Vesta's door;
Then, like a blast, away they passed,
        And no man saw them more.

XL

And all the people trembled,
    And pale grew every cheek;
And Sergius the High Pontiff
    Alone found voice to speak:
"The gods who live forever
    Have fought for Rome to-day!
These be the Great Twin Brethren
    To whom the Dorians pray.
Back comes the chief in triumph,
    Who, in the hour of fight,
Hath seen the Great Twin Brethren
    In harness on his right.
Safe comes the ship to haven,
    Through billows and through gales,
If once the Great Twin Brethren
    Sit shining on the sails.
Wherefore they washed their horses
    In Vesta's holy well,
Wherefore they rode to Vesta's door,
    I know, but may not tell.
Here, hard by Vesta's temple,
    Build we a stately dome
Unto the Great Twin Brethren
    Who fought so well for Rome.
And when the months returning
    Bring back this day of fight,
The proud Ides of Quintilis,
    Marked evermore with white,
Unto the Great Twin Brethren
    Let all the people throng,
With chaplets and with offerings,
    With music and with song;

And let the doors and windows
        Be hung with garlands all,
And let the knights be summoned
        To Mars without the wall:
Thence let them ride in purple
        With joyous trumpet-sound,
Each mounted on his war-horse,
        And each with olive crowned;
And pass in solemn order
        Before the sacred dome,
Where dwell the Great Twin Brethren
        Who fought so well for Rome!"

"What use is godlike form or mind Uncrowned by grace of speech?"

Homer, *The Odyssey*

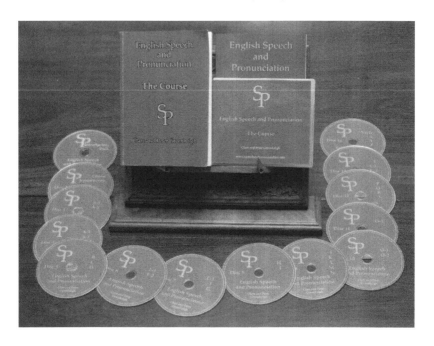

Epilogue

The two ballads you have just heard, and, we hope, enjoyed, were chosen not only to give pleasure and as good examples of the genre but also as excellent follow-up for those who have done our educational publishing company's *English Speech and Pronunciation Course*. Do practise reading these marvellous poems out loud, enjoy getting your tongue around all the glorious words and names, and let the rhythm of the verse and the pace of the story carry you along, just as Auster carried Herminius and Aulus with the speed of the South Wind, from which he was named.

The accent in which you have heard these poems read to you is the Standard English pronunciation, which is sometimes called the Received Pronunciation or the Queen's English. It is generally recognised as being the clearest and the most universally comprehensible and admired English accent not only in the United Kingdom but throughout the English-speaking world. If you do not speak with the Standard English accent and would like to learn to do so, do investigate our all-on-film *English Speech and Pronunciation* Course. It is unique in method, content and delivery, and you will find it as enjoyable as it is effective.

To find out more about this Course and about other audiobooks like this one, please visit our website, which will tell you who we are and what we do, and, most importantly, what we may be able to do for *you*! It is no exaggeration to say that we can change people's whole lives and open up unimagined opportunities professionally, socially, and culturally.

www.speechandpronunciation.com